Ripley's Believe It or Not!

WEIRD-ITIES!

Publisher Anne Marshall
Editorial Director Rebecca Miles
Assistant Editor Charlotte Howell
Text Geoff Tibballs
Proofreader Judy Barratt
Picture Researchers James Proud, Charlotte Howell
Indexer Hilary Bird
Art Director Sam South
Senior Designer Michelle Foster
Reprographics Juice Creative

Executive Vice President Norm Deska
Vice President, Archives and Exhibits Edward Meyer

PUBLISHER'S NOTE
While every effort has been made to verify the accuracy of the entries in this book, the Publishers cannot be held responsible for any errors contained in the work. They would be glad to receive any information from readers.

WARNING
Some of the stunts and activities in this book are undertaken by experts and should not be attempted by anyone without adequate training and supervision.

Published by Ripley Publishing 2013
Ripley Publishing, Suite 188, 7576 Kingspointe Parkway, Orlando, Florida 32819, USA

2 4 6 8 10 9 7 5 3 1

ISBN 978-1-60991-022-8

Some of this material first appeared in *Ripley's Believe It or Not! Expect... The Unexpected*

Library of Congress Cataloging-in-Publication data is available

Manufactured in China in July/2013
1st printing

Ripley's Believe It or Not!

WEIRD-ITIES!

LARGER THAN LIFE

RIPLEY PUBLISHING

a Jim Pattison Company

PAGE
12

PAGE
15

LARGER THAN LIFE

Out of this world. Feast your eyes on astonishing art, crazy festivals, and freaky foods. Find out about the family car that transforms into a robot, the 40-ft-long (12-m) giant surfboard, and the curious Cockroach Hall of Fame.

PAGE 26

PAGE 32

CAR-NIVOROUS

Robosaurus, a mechanical dinosaur 40 ft (12 m) tall and weighing 30 tons, is a mean machine. Dwarfing its famous predecessor T-Rex, this awesome beast can lift, crush, burn, bite, and ultimately destroy cars—and even airplanes.

Whereas T-Rex had a jaw-crushing force of 3,000 lb (1,360 kg), Robosaurus—with teeth some 12 in (30 cm) long—is seven times stronger, and can also shoot 20-ft (6-m) flames from its giant nostrils. And while T-Rex's front claws were of little use, Robosaurus's are so strong that they can crush vehicles and 50-gal (190-l) metal drums at will.

Created by American inventor Doug Malewicki in 1988 at a cost of $2.2 million, Robosaurus is controlled by a human pilot strapped inside the monster's head. The pilot initiates the robot's movements by making similar movements himself and uses foot pedals to drive Robosaurus around.

Robosaurus has appeared in movies and on TV, and has amazed spectators at live events across the U.S., Canada, and Australia.

Standing upright, Robosaurus is as high as a five-story building, dwarfing the cars parked alongside its huge frame.

Robosaurus lifts 40,000-lb (18,145-kg) cars higher than a five-story building. It crushes cars, splitting them in two, and incinerating paint and plastic. It bites and rips out roofs and doors with its fearsome stainless-steel teeth.

YOUNG ELVIS

Sal Accaputo, from Toronto, Ontario, became an Elvis impersonator at the tender age of eight. Better known as "Selvis," he has been paying tribute to the King for more than 27 years.

BABY DRIVER

When his three-year-old cousin was hurt in a fall in 2005, Tanishk Boyas drove him straight to hospital. Nothing unusual in that— except that Tanishk was only five at the time! The youngster had been learning to drive for three months at his home in India, but when he climbed into the family van it was the first time he had driven it without adult supervision. His father said, "He used to watch me drive and grasped the basics."

ICE CAP

In February 2004, 69-year-old Josef Strobl finished another of his annual ice sculptures in Italy. Strobl has been building the sculptures every year for 42 years. Some of them soar to more than 66 ft (20 m) in height. Each sculpture takes 300 hours of work, and is made of around 265,000 gal (1 million liters) of water!

WALKING TALL

In 1958, Angelo Corsaro, from Catania, Italy, walked 558 mi (898 km) to the Vatican City on wooden stilts.

PLAID CAR

Car artist Tim McNally, of Upper Montclair, New Jersey, has covered his 1985 Buick Skyhawk in plaid. He hand-painted the plaid squares on the vehicle, which also boasts beads, rhinestones, tiles, marbles, and gargoyles.

DUCK GIRL

Whenever Ruth Grace Moulon wandered through New Orleans' French Quarter, she would nearly always be followed by up to a dozen ducks. She trained the ducks to follow her everywhere and achieved local fame from the late 1950s as "The Duck Girl," charging tourists to take her photo. She called all her ducks variations on the name of Jimmy Cronin, her policeman friend.

CITIZEN CANE

Robert McKay, of Manitoba, Canada, has a collection of more than 600 wooden walking canes, each one handmade.

CORNY APPEAL

When lovelorn farmer and divorcee Pieter DeHond decided to place a personal ad, he didn't put it in a paper or magazine, but in a field. His love message came in the form of 50-ft (15-m) letters made from corn stalks on his farm at Canandaigua, New York, in 2005. Beneath the message, which took him an hour to create, an arrow 1,000 ft (305 m) long pointed females toward his house. Although the plea, measuring 900 x 600 ft (274 x 183 m), was visible only from the air, the publicity it attracted led to 700 phone calls and e-mails.

SPORTS FAN

John Carpenter, of Firebrick, Kentucky, owns more than 4,000 pieces of sports memorabilia, which include autographed baseballs, basketballs, jerseys, helmets, and letters. Best of all is the ball that Babe Ruth hit for his 552nd career home-run.

SERIOUS SURFING!

Forty-seven surfers spent 4 minutes surfing their way along the Gold Coast in Australia on March 5, 2005, on a massive surfboard 40 ft (12 m) long and 10 ft (3 m) wide—possibly the largest board ever built!

PLASTIC WRAP BALL

Andy Martell, of Toronto, Ontario, Canada, created a ball of plastic wrap that in 2003 measured 54 in (137 cm) in circumference and weighed 45 lb (20.4 kg). He made it at the Scratch Daniels restaurant, where he worked as a day cook.

MUNSTER MANSION

Something spooky has sprung up on the outskirts of Waxahachie, Texas. Charles and Sandra McKee have spent $250,000 creating a replica of the house from The Munsters TV show. Designed from set photos and TV clips, the two-story, 5,825-sq-ft (540-sq-m) house contains secret passages, Grandpa's dungeon, and a trap door leading to the quarters of Spot—the McKees' German shepherd dog, who was named after the fire-breathing dragon that the Munsters kept as a pet.

SUPERSIZE ME

Nissan Tamir, from Omer, Israel, has been growing organic vegetables for years.

In 2006 he was amazed to discover two radishes that have been growing non-stop—each one weighed a staggering 22 lb (10 kg).

LABOR OF LOVE

French postman Ferdinand Cheval spent 33 years building his Palais Idéal, or ideal castle. He began building it in 1879, collecting stones on his daily mail route, carrying them in his pockets, then in a basket, and eventually in a wheelbarrow. He often worked on the construction at night to the bemusement of his neighbors. When the authorities refused to allow him to be buried in his castle, he spent the following eight years building himself a mausoleum in the cemetery of Hautes-rives, southwest France. He finished it just in time: little over a year later, in August 1924, he died.

LUCKY'S YO-YOS

John Meisenheimer is an avid yo-yo collector. Nicknamed "Lucky," Meisenheimer began doing yo-yo tricks while on his rounds at medical school in Kentucky. His collection now stands at more than 4,250.

MENU MASTER

New Yorker Harley Spiller has his own "celebration of Chinese takeout food in America." His collection features 10,000 Chinese takeout menus, from every state in the U.S. and more than 80 countries. The oldest menu dates back to 1879. He also has an assortment of restaurant shopping bags and even a life-sized, delivery-man doll. "It's one of the nicest things you can ask a friend to do," he says, "to bring you a menu from their trip: it's lightweight and it's free."

FLYING GRANNY

In September 2002, 84-year-old grandmother Mary Murphy made the 62-mi (100-km) trip from Long Beach, California, to Catalina Island by the extreme sport of hydrofoil water-skiing. She said she wanted to make the 4-hour journey while she was still young enough.

ALIEN LANDING!

A shocked homeowner in County Durham, England, sparked a major police alert with the discovery of a slimy egg-shaped container with an alien-like fetus inside it. Detectives, forensic specialists, and a police surgeon were called before the egg-like object was identified as a child's toy.

DIAMOND IN THE SKY

Having trained for seven years, 100 skydivers from 14 countries came together to form this parachute formation shaped like a diamond. The divers linked together over Lake Wales, Florida, having only 11 minutes between the first drop and reaching the ground. They managed to hold the formation, that was the size of a jumbo jet, for 12 seconds.

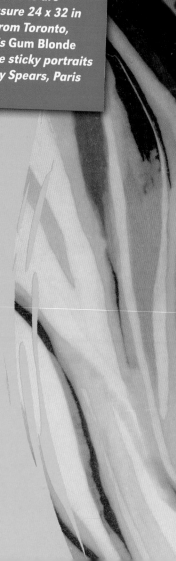

STARDATE 6.21.97

Star Trek fans Jo Ann Curl and Vince Stone had a Klingon wedding at Evansville, Indiana, in front of some 300 costumed guests. The bride wore a dark wig, a furrowed latex brow, and spoke the vows in Klingon!

HOOVER LOVERS

Founded in 1982, The Vacuum Cleaner Collectors' Club boasts around 40 American members with a passion for suction. They include Stan Kann of St. Louis, Missouri, who has a suit made of vintage vacuum-cleaner bags. He has more than 125 cleaners in his collection and can distinguish individual models by their whine and by the smell of their bags.

CHICKEN ROBBER

A man from Hillard, Ohio, robbed a grocery store while wearing a giant chicken costume!

SOLD OVER

In 1962, the Duncan Company alone sold 45 million yo-yos in the U.S., which is a country with only 40 million children!

GIANT YO-YO

In 1990, the woodwork class of Shakamak High School, Jasonville, Indiana, constructed a yo-yo that was 6 ft (1.8 m) in diameter and weighed 820 lb (372 kg). The giant yo-yo was launched from a 160-ft (49-m) crane and managed to yo-yo 12 times.

GUM BLONDES

It takes approximately 40 hours and 500 sticks of pre-chewed gum to complete one of Jason Kronenwald's Gum Blonde portraits. Kronenwald dislikes chewing gum himself, so has enlisted a team of chewers who chew a variety of flavors and colors for him—he uses no paint or dye. The portraits are made on plywood, and measure 24 x 32 in (60 x 80 cm). Kronenwald, from Toronto, Ontario, Canada, started his Gum Blonde series in 1996 and has made sticky portraits of such celebrities as Britney Spears, Paris Hilton, and Brigitte Bardot.

MANY MANEUVERS

American Hans Van Dan Helzen completed 51 different yo-yo tricks in just one minute in 2004.

YO-YO TOWN

The town of Luck, Wisconsin, was the yo-yo capital of the world during the 1940s, producing an incredible 3,600 yo-yos an hour.

BEER BELLY

Joel Freeborn, from Wauwatosa, Wisconsin, is a human bottle opener. He can open bottles of beer with his belly button!

PAC MANIA

Tim Crist, of Syracuse, New York, has a shrine to Pac Man in his home and calls himself Reverend of the First Church of Pac Man.

RHINO PARTY

For 30 years, the Canadian political scene was enlivened by a party that claimed to be the spiritual descendants of a Brazilian rhinoceros! The Rhinoceros Party was founded in 1963 by writer Jacques Ferron and contested seven federal elections without ever winning a seat. In 1980, the party declared war on Belgium after the character Tintin blew up a female rhino in a cartoon adventure!

SCALE MODEL

Models scaled the sides of the world's tallest building—the 1,667-ft (508-m) high Taipei 101 in Taiwan—for a fashion show that featured a vertical catwalk.

PET PROJECT

In 1999, in a bizarre sponsorship deal, Australian Rules footballer Gary Hocking changed his name to a pet-food brand to help his cash-strapped club. Gary became "Whiskas" in return for a donation to the club.

SPEEDY TOILET

Paul Stender's jet-powered, portable toilet on wheels can reach speeds of 40 mph (64 km/h). He races it against his friend's jet-powered bar stool!

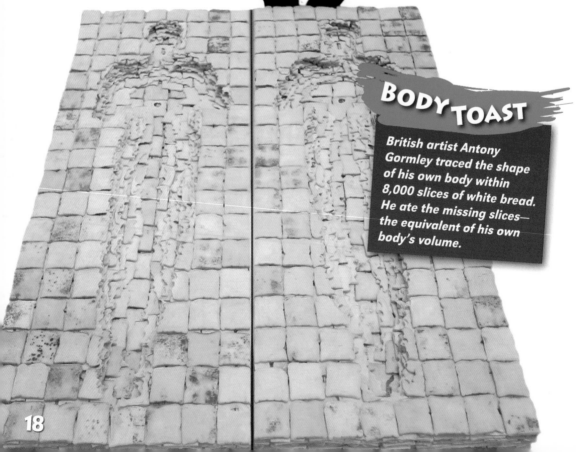

BODY TOAST

British artist Antony Gormley traced the shape of his own body within 8,000 slices of white bread. He ate the missing slices— the equivalent of his own body's volume.

ROBO-ROACH

A team of European researchers has put together a creepy-crawly robot called InsBot that behaves and smells like a cockroach and is accepted by the insects as one of their own.

LOOK WHO'S TOLKIEN

Believe it or not, American *Lord of the Rings* fan Melissa Duncan is so obsessed with the films that she takes cardboard cutouts of the characters out to dinner!

LIVING LIBRARY

In 2005, instead of lending books, a library in Malmo, Sweden, lent out humans. In an attempt to overcome common prejudices, borrowers were able to take the human items, including a homosexual, a journalist, and a blind person, for a 45-minute chat in the library's outdoor café.

BRANCHING OUT

American tree surgeon Peter Jenkins has pioneered an exhilarating new sport—extreme tree climbing. Along with other devotees, Jenkins climbs trees and performs amazing acrobatic stunts, including balancing on the branches and running across the canopy. "We also do tree surfing, where we go high into the canopy on a windy day and ride the branches. You can see the wind coming toward you in waves over the other trees."

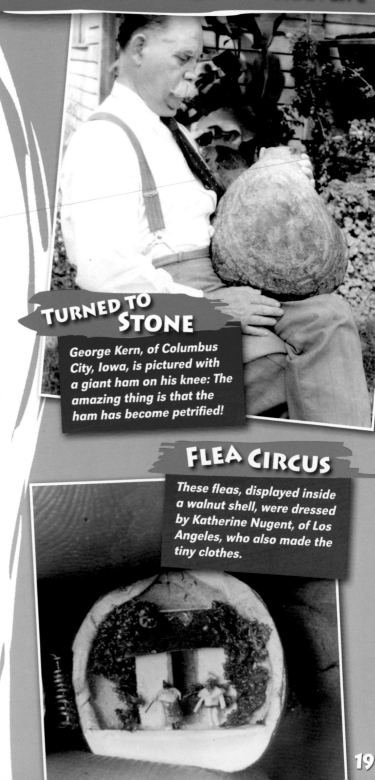

TURNED TO STONE

George Kern, of Columbus City, Iowa, is pictured with a giant ham on his knee: The amazing thing is that the ham has become petrified!

FLEA CIRCUS

These fleas, displayed inside a walnut shell, were dressed by Katherine Nugent, of Los Angeles, who also made the tiny clothes.

PEDAL POWER

Vancouver unicyclist Kris Holm, takes off-road riding to the extreme, tackling volcano craters, molten lava, and cliff tops all on one wheel.

How did you discover the unicycle?

"I saw a street performer when I was a child. He performed while playing the violin, and I had a violin too. I asked for a unicycle for my 12th birthday. I grew up doing adventure sports and rock climbing, so it was a natural progression to combine the two."

Where are the most unusual places you have ridden?

"I rode an ancient trade route in the Himalayan kingdom of Bhutan, an area very few Westerners have visited. I also rode the Great Wall of China—the security guards didn't know what to make of me. They were so surprised, they just left me alone."

Are the rides dangerous?

"I have ridden on the rail of a 200-ft-high bridge, and on the edge of an 800-m-high cliff. I have also ridden on a lava flow in the Volcanoes National Park in Hawaii—the lava had crossed a road and solidified.

It was too hot to touch but could hold my weight—I was riding within 10 m of actively flowing, red and bubbling lava."

What kind of unicycle do you use?

"A 'muni'—a mountain unicycle—is stronger than a normal unicycle, with a fatter tire. I have developed my own range—they are sold all over the world. I realized I wasn't the only one doing it when I checked the Internet by chance in the late nineties. Now there are tens of thousands of unicyclists—from Pro Skiers to Hollywood stars."

What are the hardest skills to master?

"Riding on a narrow surface, and hopping over obstacles. I can hop up to 95 cm vertically. It's also hard on the legs because you have to pedal all the time, even downhill—you can't freewheel. You can learn to take your feet off the pedals, but it's a skill, not a chance to relax. And the endurance aspect is hard—riding along the edge of a volcano crater is not technically difficult, but it is at 18,500 ft and in below-freezing temperatures."

How do you practice?

"I try to ride every day. I take a unicycle to work and ride at lunchtime. My climbing background and my day job as a geomorphologist assessing landslide risks mean I'm good at judging where a fall could kill me. You learn to ride something narrow as a coin just a metre off the ground, so when you have to ride something a foot wide but several hundred metres off the ground it feels as easy as crossing the street."

What is "competitive trials unicycling"?

"I organized the first formal trials competition for unicycles in the late nineties, and out of that grew the competitive trials. I have been a winner of the European, North American, and World trials."

Do you sustain bad injuries?

"Just lots and lots of bruises, and stitches in my chin and elbow. You don't typically fall badly—with a bicycle you fall over the handlebars head-first, whereas with a unicycle you can usually get your feet beneath you."

Where else would you like to ride?

"There are a couple of volcanoes in Bolivia I've got my eye on!"

PLAY MATE

In 2002, computer-game fan Dan Holmes officially changed his name to PlayStation 2. Holmes, from Banbury, England, played for four hours a day and had previously asked a few vicars to marry him to his console. "But none were keen," he said. "So I took its name instead."

NEWSPAPER COLLECTOR

Miao Shiming is never short of reading material at his home in China's Shanxi Province. He has collected more than 368,000 issues of over 30,000 different newspaper titles, 55,000 issues of 10,200 magazines, and 3,200 books.

SANTA PLEA

For the past four years Alan Mills, from Milford, Ohio, has been trying to change his name legally to Santa Claus— with little success. All judges have refused, just in case he uses the name for profit.

SOLAR JACKET

U.S. inventor Scott Jordan has developed a jacket that has integrated solar panels to recharge electronic gadgets in its pockets.

EVERYMAN

In 2004, Andrew Wilson, from Branson, Missouri, legally

BIG READ

This massive tome, Bhutan, A Visual Odyssey Across the Kingdom, shown in Japan in December 2003, is 5 ft (1.5 m) high and 7 ft (2.1 m) wide. Only 500 copies were published.

BEAR NECESSITIES

changed his name to "They." He says he made this unusual choice to address the common reference to "they." "They do this" or "They're to blame for that," he explained. "Who is this 'they' everyone talks about? 'They' accomplishes such great things. Somebody had to take responsibility."

BISHOP OF BROADWAY

American playwright and producer David Belasco was known as the Bishop of Broadway, because he often roamed the streets of New York dressed up as a priest.

LOVE ON A ROLLER COASTER

Angie Matthews and Steve Krist, from Puyallup, Washington, were married while riding a roller coaster!

GREEN-EYED

Ever since he was a child, Bob Green has been obsessed with the color from which his last name is derived. He lives on West Green Street, Greencastle, Indiana, invariably wears green clothes, drives a green car, and even named his three children after various shades of green—Forest, Olive, and Kelly.

A German travel agent announced in 2005 that he was offering holidays for teddy bears! Christopher Böhm said the vacations are "a great opportunity for the real man's best friend to see something different for a change." The teddies stayed in a luxury Munich apartment and spent the week sightseeing, playing games, and visiting a teddy bears' picnic and a beer house. And each bear received souvenir pictures to take home.

ELVIS ROOTS

Singer Elvis Presley's genealogical roots have been traced back to Lonmay, Scotland, where a new tartan was created in his honor.

YOUNG DOCTOR

In 1995, Balamurali Ambati graduated from the Mount Sinai School of Medicine, New York City, aged just 17. The average age for graduates from medical school is 26 or 27. Despite his young age, his first patients didn't realize they were being treated by a teenager—at 6 ft (1.8 m) tall, they thought he was much older.

OLDEST SCHOOLBOY

Kimani Maruge stands out from his classmates at Kapkenduiywa primary school in Kenya, for he is twice the height and 17 times the age of most of his fellow pupils. The 85-year-old student sits with his long legs folded under the

tiny desk during classes. He is also the only pupil at the school to wear a hearing aid and carry a walking stick.

PREMIUM BOND

Matt Sherman thinks he's a real-life James Bond. He spends his spare time practicing survival techniques near his home in Gainesville, Florida, and turns routine shopping trips into pretend MI6 missions in which his two young children are given assignments to fetch certain

groceries within a specified time. A collector of 007 memorabilia for more than 20 years, he has turned his den into a shrine to James Bond, complete with books, jewelry, and even Cologne relating to his hero. He has also spent more than $10,000 on spy equipment that he uses for monitoring purposes.

KLINGON PIZZA

American Star Trek fan Shane Dison is obsessed with being a Klingon! He makes sure that his daily diet includes Mexican-style pizzas, because

they're the closest things to Klingon food on Earth.

SLEEPY TRAVELER

Tom Wilson, of Los Angeles, California, is the first person to "sleep across America." He toured the country in a chauffered Winnebago that traveled only while he was fast asleep.

GAME'S UP

Devoted baseball fan Joe Vitelli, of Westborough, Massachusetts, was so desperate to watch game seven of the New York Yankees–Boston Red Sox American League Championship series in 2003 that he faked a broken leg in order to get out of attending his girlfriend's sorority formal on the same day. He even wore a fake cast for six weeks, used a wheelchair, and "attended" various bogus doctor's appointments before he was spotted walking—and the game was up!

BUMPER HORSE

This sculpture of a mustang horse was made by Sean Guerrero, of Colorado, from stainless-steel car bumpers. It stands nearly 14 ft (4.3 m) high and weighs several thousand pounds.

BLOWING BUBBLES

Fan Yang can do just about anything with bubbles. He has created bubbles within bubbles, smoking bubbles, and spinning, bouncing, floating bubbles of every imaginable size, shape, and color.

In 2004, Fan Yang managed to fit 15 people in a bubble at the Santa Ana Discovery Science Center, California.

In Seattle, Washington, in 1997, the Canadian bubble enthusiast created an amazing bubble wall that measured 156 ft (47.5 m) long and 13 ft (4 m) high—the equivalent of walking onto a football field and forming a giant bubble from the end zone to the 50-yard line. Three years later, he built a bubble so sturdy that his daughter was able to slide into a bubble hemisphere without bursting the film.

In 2001, Yang managed to arrange 12 bubbles inside each other; and in the same year, in Stockholm, Sweden, he interlinked nine bubbles to make one long chain that floated in mid-air.

Fan Yang has dedicated the past 20 years to developing the art of bubbles. His skill has been recognized by science centers all over the world, and was born out of a childhood fascination with bubbles.

CEREAL DEVOTION

Roger Barr, of Richmond, Virginia, has been dedicating his life to saving Boo Berry cereal from extinction. He is so devoted to the product that he has set up an Internet fan site and even hides rival brands on supermarket shelves in the hope of slowing their sales. And he's not alone. One woman once drove a staggering 26,000 mi (41,845 km) to get her hands on a packet of Boo Berry.

CRACKPOT KING

In 2003, plain Nick Copeman changed his name officially to H.M. King Nicholas I. Calling himself "Britain's other monarch," he rode on horseback in full uniform through his home town of Sheringham, Norfolk, sold nobility titles over the Internet, and started the Copeman Empire from his royal palace, which was, in fact, a two-berth caravan.

OFF HIS TROLLEY

An inventive designer has been turning Britain's unwanted supermarket carts into furniture. About 100,000 old carts are destroyed in Britain every year, but Colin Lovekin, from Exeter, Devon, has come up with a new use for them. He has been turning them into chairs and sofas, complete with cushioned seating, wheeled legs, and even a basket at the back.

MONSTER BALL

While working in the post room of a law firm near his home in Wilmington, Delaware, John Bain had to collect mail from the post office every day. At the post office he would routinely grab a handful of free rubber bands, which he then made into a ball. Five years and two months later, the monster ball, made up of 850,000 rubber bands, weighed 3,120 lb (1,415 kg), stood 5 ft (1.5 m) high, and had a circumference of 15 ft (4.6 m). Bain estimated that it would have cost him $25,000 to make.

SLINGSHOT LOBES

Nicknamed "Slingshot Ears," Monte Pierce uses his amazingly long earlobes to launch coins distances of up to 10 ft (3 m)! Pierce, from Bowling Green, Kentucky, began tugging on his earlobes when he was young, not only increasing their length but also their ability to snap back. His lobes permanently hang down an inch (2.5 cm), but for his launches he can stretch them to 5 in (13 cm). He can also pull them up over his eyes and can even roll them up and stuff them into his ears.

WASTE ENERGY

The methane in cow dung collected at the Blue Spruce Farm in Bridport, Vermont, produces enough electricity to power 330 homes!

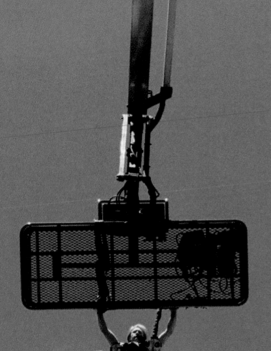

WALKING TALL

Jeff Jay has taken the art of stilt walking to extremes—he is able to walk on stilts that are 60 ft (18 m) tall. They were specially designed and created by him, and require a crane in order to get on to them!

TRANSFORMER!

Brazilian Olésio da Silva and his two sons Marcus Vinicius and Marco Aurelio have teamed up to create a life-size robocar. They transformed their Kia Besta van into a 12-ft (3.7-m) robot that plays loud music as it transforms. It cost them $122,000 and takes 6 minutes to transform.

TATTOO TRIBUTE

Dan Summers, from Thompsonville, Illinois, is a living tribute to *The Three Stooges*. He has tattoos of Larry, Moe, and Curly covering his entire body, including his face.

CRAZY CRAFT

How about sailing down the river in an electric wheelchair or in a two-seater pedal-powered floating tricycle? Well, wacky inventor Lyndon Yorke, of Buckinghamshire, England, can make your dreams come true. Among his ingenious seaworthy designs are the tricycle (the *PP Tritanic*) and the *Tritania*, a 1920s wheelchair complete with wind-up gramophone, Champagne cooler, and picnic basket.

SURFING MICE

Australian surfing enthusiast Shane Willmott has been training three mice to surf small waves on tiny mouse-sized surfboards at beaches on the Gold Coast. The mice—Harry, Chopsticks, and Bunsen—live in miniature custom-made villas and own specially made jet skis. They train in a bathtub and then have their fur dyed when it's time to hit the beach. Willmott explains: "Because they're white, when they get in the whitewash of big waves, it's hard to find them."

AMERICAN PATRIOT

Ski Demski was the ultimate patriot. He owned a Stars and Stripes flag that measured 505 x 225 ft (154 x 68.6 m), weighed 3,000 lb (1,360 kg), and took 600 people to unfurl. Each star was 17 ft (5 m) high. He also had a tattoo of Old Glory on his chest. Before his death in 2002, Demski ran unsuccessfully for mayor of Long Beach, California, whenever there was an election.

KISSING COBRAS

Gordon Cates, of Alachua, Florida, kisses cobras for fun. The owner of more than 200 reptiles, he says that he can anticipate the snakes' actions by reading their body language.

BARKING MAD

Believe it or not, animal behaviorist Jill Deringer, from Lantana, Florida, can mimic the distinctive barks of 261 different breeds of dog!

LAST REQUEST

Before his suicide in February 2005, popular American writer Hunter S. Thompson asked to be cremated and to have his ashes fired from a cannon. Accordingly, his remains shot into the sky six months later from a 153-ft (47-m) tower behind his home in Woody Creek, Colorado.

ROLLER-COASTER RIDE

During the 2005 summer vacation, a 14-year-old boy, from Offenburg, Germany, built a roller coaster in his backyard that was 300 ft (91 m) long. He even designed his own carriage, which was able to reach speeds of up to 30 mph (48 km/h) on the 16-ft (5-m) high wooden construction.

GIANT STOCKING

In 2004, J. Terry Osborne and friends, from King William County, Virginia, created a Christmas stocking more than 35 ft (10.7 m) high and 16½ ft (5 m) wide. It was filled with presents for children in need.

ELVIS IMPERSONATOR

New Yorker Mike Memphis will go to any lengths to look like his hero Elvis Presley. An Elvis impersonator since the age of 16, Mike underwent several facial procedures on Elvis's birthday in 1994 so that he could look more like the King. The multiple operations comprised liposuction of the face, cheek implants, a lower-lip implant, a chin implant, liposuction of the neck and chin, and implants on both sides of his jaw.

CRAWL TO WORK

A lifeguard from Essex, England, has hit upon the perfect way to avoid rush-hour traffic—by swimming to work. Each morning, 45-year-old Martin Spink walks down to the beach near his home, checks the tides, strips down to his shorts and flippers, and swims across Brightlingsea Creek. Ten minutes later, he emerges on the other side, pulls a clothes bag from his back, and dresses for work.

He does it to save a 20-mi (32-km) round trip by road from home to his workplace.

ON TOP OF THE WORLD

In May 2005, a Nepalese couple became the first to be wed on top of the world's highest mountain, Mount Everest. Moments after reaching the summit, Mona Mulepati and Pem Dorje Sherpa briefly took off their oxygen masks, donned plastic garlands, and exchanged marriage vows. The only witness was the third member of the party, Kami Sherpa.

SUPER SAVER

Roy Haynes, from Huntington, Vermont, prides himself on being the cheapest man in the world. He splits his two-ply toilet paper into two rolls of one-ply, and dries out and reuses paper towels over and over again. He also saves money by taking ketchup packets from restaurants and squeezing them into his own ketchup bottle at home.

STAIR CLIMB

In September 2002, Canadian Paralympian Jeff Adams became the first person to climb the 1,776 stairs of Toronto's CN Tower in a wheelchair. It took him seven hours, moving backwards up the steps.

BIG DIFFERENCE

The world's smallest teen met the man with the biggest biceps in Britain at the Ripley's Believe it or Not! museum in London, England, in September 2010. Khagendra Thapa Magar, 17, from the Baglung District of Nepal, measures just 22 inches (56 cm) in height, barely the size of a toddler, and Tiny Iron, a 28-year-old bodyguard from London, has biceps that are bigger in circumference than Khagendra is tall!

HEAVYWEIGHT

Hercules is a three-year-old liger. An "accident," his father is a lion and his mother is a tiger. Standing 10 ft (3 m) tall on his back legs, he already weighs more than 900 lb (408 kg) and is still growing. Hercules consumes 20 lb (9 kg) of meat a day, usually chicken and beef, but can manage to eat 100 lb (45 kg) in one meal. This amazing animal is as strong as a lion and as fast as a tiger, reaching speeds of 50 mph (80 km/h)!

COCKROACH CELEBRITIES

Pestkiller Michael Bohdan has a love-hate relationship with his pests—he has killed thousands, but has also made a permanent feature out of his best catches in the Cockroach Hall of Fame.

After launching a stunt to find Dallas's largest cockroach, pest-control specialist Michael Bohdan was left with the problem of what to do with the dead bodies. Instead of throwing them out, he decided to dress them up as celebrities—and the Cockroach Hall of Fame Museum was born.

Each year, thousands of curious customers visit the museum in Plano, Texas, to catch a glimpse of such heroes in a half shell as H. Ross Peroach, David Letteroach, Marilyn Monroach, and, seated at a tiny piano and wearing a white cape, the inimitable Liberoachi.

Marilyn Monroach in her famous white dress.

"Liberoachi" poised for his performance.

SECRET THRONE

Following the death of janitor James Hampton in 1964, it emerged that for the previous 14 years he had been building a secret throne from scavenged materials in a rented garage in Washington, D.C. The glittering throne was made from silver and gold foil, old furniture, pieces of cardboard, old light bulbs, shards of mirror, and old desk blotters. He had pinned the magnificent chair together with tacks, glue, pins, and tape. The throne, with its biblical messages, was later donated to the National Museum of American Art.

STATE NAMES

The former editor of The Wall Street Journal was named Vermont Connecticut Royster. Indeed, his great-grandfather called his sons Iowa Michigan, Arkansas Delaware, Wisconsin Illinois, and Oregon Minnesota; while the girls were Louisiana Maryland, Virginia Carolina, and Georgia Indiana!

BASEBALL BOY

Zach Spedden called an entire nine-inning baseball game on radio station WHAG 1410 AM, in Hagerstown, Maryland, in 2002, when he was ten years old. He also presented the pre-game show and the post-game analysis. It had been his ambition since the age of five.

APPLE OF YOUR EYE

Emma Karp and her father Helge Lundstrom have been making giant apple mosaics since 1988 for the Kivik Apple Market in Sweden. Some of their creations include as many as 75,000 apples in 15 different varieties—that's 8,820 lb (4,000 kg) in weight!

AND THEY'RE OFF!

The first Office Chair World Championships took place in Olten, Switzerland, on June 11, 2005. The race, which was 650 ft (200 m) long, saw 64 competitors from Germany, France, and Switzerland take part.

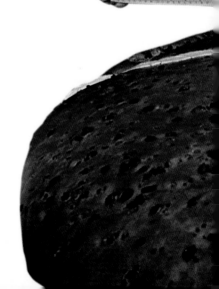

HEMINGWAY DAYS

The highlight of the annual Hemingway Days' festival in Key West, Florida, is the Ernest Hemingway look-alike contest. The event attracts national and international entrants, who dress themselves up in fishermen's wool turtlenecks and other sporting attire, and make their way to Sloppy Joe's Bar—Hemingway's favorite watering hole when he lived in Key West in the 1930s. Beating off 146 white-bearded, ruddy-faced rivals to snatch the coveted title in 2005 was 61-year-old Bob Doughty, a letter-carrier from Deerfield Beach, Florida.

HIGH CHURCH

In August 2003, ten couples took their wedding vows in mid-air aboard an airplane flying from Orlando, Florida, to Las Vegas, Nevada. Fittingly for such a bizarre occasion, the in-flight ceremony was conducted by a minister dressed as Elvis Presley.

GINGER NINJA

From his nickname, you could guess that "Orange" Mike Lowrey, of Milwaukee, Wisconsin, wears nothing but orange. He is usually seen out and about in an orange hat, orange shirt, orange belt, orange pants, orange sneakers, and orange wristwatch band. "It's no big deal," he insists. "I just like the color orange."

UNDERWATER WEDDING

Chandan Thakur and Dipti Pradhan's wedding took place underwater in June 2003 at the Vashi Marine Centre on Thailand's Kradan Island. First, diving instructor Ravi Kulkami conducted the engagement as the couple exchanged rings while suspended by ropes 50 ft (15 m) above the Vashi

pool. Then, 11 days later, Kulkami, the bride and groom, and seven relatives dived under the water for the 30-minute ceremony. The couple had metal strips sewn into the hems of their wedding outfits so that they kept their shape in the water.

OLD PLAYER

At 96, Henry Paynter was still a regular player at Kelowna Badminton Club, British Columbia, traveling to games across the region. He died in April 2005, aged 98.

BIG EASTER BUNS

Baker Brian Collins proudly shows off his giant hot cross bun at Pegrum's Bakery in Rustington, England. His bun measured more than 48 in (122 cm) in diameter.

ALL TAPED UP

Certified
DUCT TAPE
PRO

Wisconsin brothers-in-law Tim Nyberg and Jim Berg, are the Duct Tape Guys—they have collected well over 5,000 uses for the product and say there's virtually nothing it can't fix.

Tim, when did you first develop your passion for duct tape?

"We were at Jim's sister's home for Christmas in 1993 and a storm caused a power outage. Jim said, 'If I knew where that power outage originated, I could probably fix it with duct tape.' His wife agreed, 'Jim fixes everything with duct tape!' They rattled off a few of his recent fixes, and I thought, 'There's a book here!' So we all sat around in the candlelight brainstorming uses for duct tape. By the end of the day, we had 365 uses listed."

How did you become the Duct Tape Guys?

"Back home, I illustrated and designed a book and sent it off to a few publishers. One acquisitions editor who happened to be familiar with duct tape humor from his college years pulled it out of the reject pile and convinced his editor by duct taping him into his chair until he agreed to publish it. That was seven books and close to three million copies ago. I have a background in stand-up comedy, and Jim is naturally funny, so we created the Duct Tape Guys to provide interviewable characters to accompany our books."

What are some of the strangest uses for duct tape?

"A dermatologist wrote us about nine years ago saying he successfully treated warts by simply adhering a strip of duct tape over the wart until it died. No chemicals needed. Five or six years later, there was a medical white paper written about the same treatment. Now people send us their wart testimonials. Jim's personal favorite use is duct taping his television remote control to his arm so he doesn't lose it (and doesn't have to relinquish remote use to his wife and kids)."

Why is it so well-loved?

"It's a quick fix. It needs no directions, so there is no limit to one's creativity. It's extremely versatile. By folding it over onto intself two or three times it's strong enough to pull a car out of a ditch, yet you can rip it with your bare hands. Enough duct tape is sold each year to stretch to the moon 1.2 times. We've even heard of funerals where families have honored grandpa's fondness of duct tape by giving each family member a little strip of tape to seal the coffin."

Does anything else come close?

"We have two tools in our tool box. A roll of duct tape and a can of WD-40®. There are two rules that get you through life: If it's not stuck and it's supposed to be, duct tape it. If it's stuck and it's not supposed to be, WD-40 it."

Is there anything you can't do with duct tape?

"That's the leading question in our seventh book, 'Stump the Duct Tape Guys.' The question that finally stumped us was, 'How do you stop somebody who loves duct tape from using only duct tape?' We have no idea. Give someone more duct tape and they love it all the more, finding more and more uses for the stuff. Take it away and the heart only grows fonder."

PARTY ANIMAL

American financier George A. Kessler loved parties. In 1905, he threw a birthday party at London's Savoy Hotel with a Venetian theme. He had the hotel courtyard flooded with blue-dyed water to simulate a canal and, against a painted backdrop, his two dozen guests sat inside a vast silk-lined gondola, served by waiters dressed as gondoliers and serenaded by opera singer Enrico Caruso. Kessler's birthday cake was 5 ft (1.5 m) high and arrived strapped to the back of a baby elephant, which was led across a gangplank to the gondola.

FOUR-YEAR FAST

In May 2005, German scientist Dr. Michael Werner announced that he had eaten nothing for the previous four years. He said he drank only water mixed with a little fruit juice and claimed to get all his energy from sunlight.

QUIRKY CASTLE

While both his parents were out at work one day, 17-year-old Howard Solomon ripped the back wall off their new suburban home and started adding on a porch. Now his parents live in a back room of their son's home—a castle in a central Florida swamp. That early brush with homebuilding inspired Solomon's love for grand creations. He began his castle at Ona in 1972 and it now covers 12,000 sq ft (1,115 sq m) and stands three stories high. The exterior is covered in shiny aluminum printing plates, discarded by the local weekly newspaper, and the interior is home to his quirky sculptures, including a gun that shoots toilet plungers.

INFLATABLE ALARM

Chilean inventors Miguel Angel Peres and Pedro Galvez created the "Good Awakening Pillow," a device originally intended as an alarm clock for the deaf. The pillow very gently shakes the owner's head by slowly inflating and deflating.

HOWZAT!

A cricket ball, made in Sri Lanka, boasts 2,704 diamonds, and is claimed to be the first life-size diamond-and-gold cricket ball.

SCORCHER

Dr. Bunhead, a.k.a. Tom Pringle, is a teacher with a difference. He tries to bring science alive to both old and young by making it exciting—mainly with big bangs. His feats include firing eight potatoes from a potato launcher in 3 minutes and setting light to his head.

PLAYING WITH FIRE

Believe it or not, Steve Truglia encourages people to set him on fire! Britain's top fire stuntman has appeared in many films and TV shows burning from head to toe at temperatures of around 800°F (425°C).

Steve often performs these stunts without oxygen and can hold his breath for more than two minutes while on fire. "Breathing is not an option," he explains, adding that one gasp of air would almost certainly be his last. Steve is also planning to break his present record for the longest time spent totally on fire. His current best is 2 minutes 5 seconds.

As a professional stuntman, he has been blown up, crushed, thrown down flights of steps, and "killed" more times than he can remember. To improve road safety, he also acts as a human crash test dummy, deliberately driving cars into aluminum highway signs at speeds of more than 60 mph (96 km/h)—and walking away unharmed.

In 2004, Steve performed over 50 full body burns—more than most stunt people do in an entire career.

Steve can hold his breath for 6 minutes 10 seconds underwater, something that stands him in good stead for many of his burning stunts, but he is also able to conceal an air supply for longer stunts.

FACE-OFF

Sculptor Ron Mueck exhibited his work—a lifelike sleeping face—in the Museum of Contemporary Art in Sydney, Australia, in 2002. A self-portrait, it is made from a fiberglass resin and is part of a collection of "hyper-real" figures made by the artist.

BROOKLYN MISER

Henrietta Howland Green was one of the world's richest women. She had more than $31 million in one bank account alone, yet she lived a frugal life in a seedy Brooklyn apartment where the heating remained firmly switched off—even in the depths of winter. Her lunch was a tin of dry oatmeal, which she heated on the radiator at her bank. She never bothered to wash and usually wore the same frayed old black dress. Tied around her waist with string was a battered handbag containing cheap broken biscuits. When she died in 1916, she left an estate worth $100 million.

MUG MAESTRO

Since 1972, Harold Swauger, an enthusiastic mug collector from New Philadelphia, Ohio, has collected more than 4,500 examples from all over the world.

CHIMP MARRIAGE

After flirting through the bars of their respective enclosures for four months, two chimpanzees were married at a Brazilian zoo in 2003 in an attempt to encourage them to breed. The "couple" at Rio de Janeiro Zoo wore wedding gowns for the ceremony and had their own wedding cake.

ACKNOWLEDGMENTS

FRONT COVER (t/l) Keith MacBeth, (b/l) Nino Fernando Campagna, (sp) Azulai/Rex Features; 4 (l) Azulai/Rex Features, (r) Keith MacBeth; 5 (l) Nino Fernando Campagna; 6–7 www.robosaurus.com; 8 Joe Klamar/AFP/Getty Images; 10–11 Steve Holland/AP/PA Photos; 12–13 Azulai/Rex Features; 14 Owen Humphreys/PA Archive/PA Photos; 15 Keith MacBeth; 17 Jason Kronenwald; 18 Reuters/Toby Melville; 20 www.seanwhite.net; 22 Toru Yamanaka/AFP/Getty Images; 23 Sam Barcroft/Barcroft Media; 26–27 Nino Fernando Campagna; 29 Paul Ortiz; 30 Barcroft Media; 33 Sam Barcroft/Barcroft Media; 34–35 Matt Slocum/AP/PA Photos; 36–37 Thorsten Persson/Barcroft Media; 38 Reuters/Sebastian Derungs; 39 Chris Ison/PA Archive/PA Photos; 40 Octane Creative; 42 Sena Vidanagama/AFP/Getty Images; 43 Andrew Jeffery; 44–45 Sam Barcroft/Barcroft Media; 46–47 Reuters/David Gray

KEY t = top, b = bottom, c = center, l = left, r = right, sp = single page, dp = double page

All other photos are from Ripley's Entertainment Inc.
Every attempt has been made to acknowledge correctly and contact copyright holders and we apologize in advance for any unintentional errors or omissions, which will be corrected in future editions.